PERSONALITY ASSETS®

TOOLS FOR GETTING THE JOB

LESLIE MACOMBER, MBA

Copyright © 2013 by Leslie Macomber.
All rights reserved.
Personality Assets® is a registered trademark.

Leslie Macomber
P.O. Box 102
Coeur d'Alene, ID 83816

ISBN-10: 1480177873
ISBN-13: 9781480177871
LCCN: 2012920444
CreateSpace Independent Publishing Platform
North Charleston, South Carolina

For information about Online Curriculum, sponsoring a
Personality Assets® seminar, or One-on-One Job Coach services,
go to PersonalityAssets.com.

No part of this book may be reproduced in any form, or by any electronic or mechanical means including information storage and retrieval systems, without written permission from the author. The only exception is by a reviewer, who may quote short excerpts in a review.

TABLE OF CONTENTS

Acknowledgments v
Introduction. vii
Chapter 1: Soft Skills and the Power of Chemistry 1
Chapter 2: Personality Assets 5
Chapter 3: The FAB in *You!* 11
Chapter 4: Individual Personality Assets 19
Chapter 5: Social Personality Assets 23
Chapter 6: Leadership Personality Assets 25
Chapter 7: Turn a Weakness into a Strength 27
Chapter 8: Your Elevator Pitch 33
Chapter 9: Advanced Personality Assets:
　　　　　　 Any Questions?. 37
Chapter 10: Bringing It All Together:
　　　　　　　The Job Interview .41
Chapter 11: Your Mock Job Interview 53
Final Thoughts 57
Appendix: Personality Assets 59
Glossary. 61
About the Author 65

ACKNOWLEDGMENTS

The experience I've gained over my ten years as an Executive Recruiter is the basis for this book. Recruiters often develop a level of professional intimacy with their recruits, and are privileged with insights about the search process seldom shared otherwise. The information in this book is gleaned from the many highly intelligent, conscientious, and hard-working professionals I have had the privilege of working with over the years. It is hoped that the distillation of this shared experience will benefit the readers of this book.

If there is one person responsible for the existence of this book, it is Cheryl Taylor. She provided support from the beginning, and perspicacious advice along the way.

The burden of tolerance for the time devoted to this text falls on my husband, Arthur, without whom I am nothing. He has a keen editing eye, and the imaginative methods of presenting the material are his. My two children, Jessie and Ben, have missed dinners and put up with a highly distracted mother as their sacrifice to the cause.

Debbie, James, and Logan Clelland pitched in with support and feedback at a critical time when I was not certain this book's contents had a place outside of my imagination. Chris and Dana Belstler contributed constructive feedback and lots of "go getums." Mark Boone stepped in as editor midway through the project to provide structure. Jeff Hill and Terri Boyd-Davis have given valuable feedback as well.

"He" and "she" are used in the text, rather than "you" and "they." This is a stylistic choice meant to personalize the text. No preference is intended to be given to either sex.

Material from the film *Being Flynn* (2012) is used with the permission of Focus Features, a division of NBC Universal.

Finally, if the reader of this book finds sustenance in its pages, it is to the grace of the Almighty that praise should be given.

INTRODUCTION

You're in the middle of a job interview. When asked, "Why should I hire you?" you react like a deer caught in the headlights. Your mouth gets dry and your mind goes blank. You ask yourself, "Yeah, why would you hire me?"

Job seekers are notoriously unprepared to address interview questions regarding their basic strengths and motivations. In the movie *"Being Flynn,"* adapted from the 2004 memoir by Nick Flynn, Nick interviews for a job at a homeless shelter. When asked, "Why do you want to work with homeless people?" Nick offers an honest but problematic answer saying, "I don't know. I guess I wanna job that means something, where at the end of the day I don't despise myself." To his credit, Nick avoided the routine mistake of offering a canned answer, but he unintentionally took the interview in an unproductive direction. Nick's answer to the interviewer's next question, "So you despise yourself?" didn't restore confidence in his candidacy and he was rejected for the job.

Later, Nick is given a second chance at the job on a trial basis. During the on-the-job trial, he performs well and is eventually made a permanent employee. He goes on to be successful in the position, even under stressful circumstances, proving that he had the right stuff the whole time. What if Nick had been prepared initially to convince his interviewer that he was the right candidate? What if he had said:

> "I'm at a point in my life where I want to reach out and be helpful to others. I feel like I have something to contribute to people's lives and, at the end of the day, I think this job would make me feel good about myself."

Odds are that he would have been offered the job the first time.

As a practicing recruiter, this author has watched hundreds of qualified, intelligent, conscientious job seekers rejected for jobs they were competent to perform, simply because they were unprepared to convince their interviewer they were the *right* person or *best* candidate. Self-confidence turns to self-doubt in the face of multiple rejections. Unlike Nick, most candidates don't get a second chance.

When you are at your best during the interview, the likelihood of getting the job increases. What is less well recognized is that when you are at your best but don't get the job, rejection is easier to accept, because it's clear that the match was not meant to be. Best to be prepared, perform well, and avoid regret.

How This Book Is Organized

This book is divided into eleven chapters. Chapters 1 and 2 address the analytical framework of the book. Chapters 3 through 9 introduce you to the "tools" critical for personalizing your answers to today's important interview questions. Chapter 10 applies the concepts of the book to a theoretical interview and in Chapter 11 you practice using your tools during a mock interview. The Appendix includes the complete list of Personality Assets. The book ends with a glossary for your reference.

Starting with Chapter 2, there are exercises at the end of each Chapter. These exercises are your chance to practice the Personality Assets tools and make them yours. Getting to your "A-game" is like learning to ride a bicycle ... it takes practice! But, like riding a bike, once you learn you never forget. The tools of Personality Assets will stay with you for a lifetime, helping you assess developing strengths and sell them to skeptical listeners. Practice the material in this book until it is second nature to gain maximum benefit.

Chapter 1

SOFT SKILLS AND THE POWER OF CHEMISTRY

In a competitive hiring environment where dozens of job seekers compete for one position, it isn't enough to be qualified to perform the basic demands of the job. When hiring managers have their pick of candidates with the right "hard skills"—measurable skills gained by education, training, or experience—the candidate's ability to get the job done is taken for granted. The winning candidate needs the right hard skills *plus more.*

The old adage about getting a job, "It's all about the chemistry," is as true today as it's ever been. Interpersonal "chemistry" is hard to explain, but everyone knows it when they experience it. When people meet and "hit it off," it's said they have chemistry. In a job interview, chemistry happens when an interviewer sees that a candidate is not only capable of performing the job, but has something else the organization values, something not found on a resume or application.

During the job interview, chemistry happens when the *soft skills* of the job candidate match the *soft needs* of the organization. Soft skills are valuable personality characteristics that can't be seen or measured, but are real nonetheless. A soft skill can be as basic as a can-do attitude or as complex as being politically savvy.

Think of the people you care about and what makes them special. They may be funny, forthright, empathic, easygoing, have a way with words, or care about you in a special way. All of these characteristics are soft skills. Soft skills are what make human beings *human*. They are the words we use to describe our family, friends, coworkers, and acquaintances. Soft skills are what make us likeable or not, easy to work with or not, productive or not. Even though soft skills aren't included on an application or resume, they exist and they are *real*.

There are lots of soft skills. If you went through a dictionary and found all the words that describe soft skills, you'd find that there are literally thousands. When you realize that each of us has hundreds, perhaps thousands, of soft skills, you start to see why people are so different. Try to imagine all the possible combinations of these thousands of soft skills, and your brain will short-circuit! Mathematically speaking, as the number of soft skills goes up, the number of unique combinations of those skills increases exponentially, meaning that the probability that any two people possess the same combination is practically zero.

Since your combination of soft skills is unique, you have what no other job candidate has -- *You! You!* are your candidacy's creative core, its motivation, and its energy. *You!* create its content and give it shape. *You!* give your job search direction.

And, finally, *You!* are what makes chemistry happen during the job interview.

This book equips you to identify what makes you *You!* Give your interviewer the information she needs to hire you by providing authentic answers to today's most important interview questions.

* * *

Before you get to the interview, your candidacy exists in one dimension only: the information contained on your resume or application. You were granted the interview based on hard skill information that can be quantified, certified, or described in writing, such as experience, education, training, and honors.

When you arrive at the interview, a second dimension is added to your candidacy: your physical presence. Your interviewer observes your physical attributes like height, weight, posture, speech, facial expressions, choice of dress, and body language.

As you progress through the interview, the third and most important dimension is added: soft skills. Your interviewer asks questions about your strengths and weaknesses, your motivation for wanting the position, your career goals, and generally assesses how your soft skills will match the soft needs of the organization. This is the make-or-break part of the interview! When your interviewer recognizes that you have the right combination of hard and soft skills, he will *see* you performing successfully in the job, getting along with the work team, and contributing to the goals of the organization. When chemistry kicks in, your interviewer commits to your candidacy and mentally moves one step closer to job offer.

PERSONALITY ASSETS

Although no one expects fireworks during the job interview, the process of moving past the interview stage to job offer is an emotional one governed by the laws of interpersonal chemistry. Use your soft skills to convince your interviewer that you are the right candidate for the job.

Chapter 2

PERSONALITY ASSETS

So far, the discussion of soft skills has been broad and inclusive. In the last chapter, we noted that there are thousands of valuable soft skills. However, for the purpose of the job interview, not all soft skills are equal. It turns out that many, if not most, soft skills are irrelevant to the soft needs of the workplace. For example, it's difficult to imagine a traditional workplace where the soft skills "spiritual" or "soulful" would be critical to success in the job. However highly these soft skills might be valued in other facets of life, it's simply unlikely they would be valued enough to lead to a job offer. For the purpose of preparing for the job interview, our attention will be limited to those soft skills that are relevant to the workplace. This is where Personality Assets steps in.

Personality Assets are defined as soft skills that are relevant to the workplace, are highly descriptive, and are valuable.

(See the Appendix for a complete list.) Examples are "disciplined," "cooperative," and "motivating."

Personality Assets includes soft skills relevant to job seekers with no experience all the way through candidates with many years experience, including management. Examples of Personality Assets relevant to first-time job seekers are "good attitude," "hard-working," and "honest." Assets relevant to more experienced workers depend on the nature of the candidate's experience, but could include "innovative," "independent," and "self-starter." These are just a few examples of the many soft skills that make you stand out from the crowd. Job offers hinge on convincing a potential employer that you own the soft skills they value most.

Given the inexact nature of soft skills, there is no science behind which soft skills rise to the level of Personality Assets. Personality Assets is best viewed as a reliable list of valuable soft skills relevant to the workplace, but not as an exhaustive list.

* * *

Personality Assets are divided into three dimensions: Individual, Social, and Leadership. Each dimension addresses a qualitatively different aspect of work life where personality assets are relevant.

The *Individual* dimension is the largest and reflects not just the diversity of ways that individuals contribute to a work environment, but also the importance of the individual's contribution to the work product. The individual dimension includes personality assets that describe an individual's work product, ethic, attitude, orientation, style, motivation, and character.

The *Social* dimension addresses the psychically interrelated nature of work, and the fact that work is most often done in a group or team setting. The ability to develop productive relationships with juniors, peers, and seniors in a hierarchy is essential to success on most jobs. The social dimension includes personality assets that describe interaction style, social skills, communication skills, and how you relate with coworkers.

The *Leadership* dimension addresses the reality that groups require direction and motivation to be productive. Although the qualities of leaders are undoubtedly as varied, multi-dimensional, and complex as the situations they are found in, at the most fundamental level leaders motivate and productively direct the resources and activities of groups. The personality assets chosen for this dimension reflect these qualities.

* * *

Ironically, as critical as personality assets are to getting the job, they are not typically included on a resume or job application. The most obvious reason for this is that personality assets are difficult to describe in writing because you can't see or measure them. So, rather than risk being interpreted in the wrong way, job applicants shy away from making assertions that can easily be misinterpreted. Secondly, the inclusion of personality assets on a resume or job application runs the risk of sounding boastful. Simply *saying* you're a hard worker on a resume or job application won't go far in convincing a skeptical reader that you actually *are* a hard worker. The skeptical mind responds, "Give me a reason why I should believe you're a hard worker," something that neither resume nor job application can substantively address. Either of these reasons is sufficient for omitting personality assets on a resume or job application.

Clearly, the job interview is your best opportunity to convince an interviewer that you own your personality assets. The two-way communication, the back and forth between interviewer and interviewee, is ideal for the presentation of your personality assets. Make your interviewer "see" your asset in action and "feel" its impact in your life during the interview and you have sold them on its authenticity. When your interviewer knows in their gut that what you say is true, they move from skeptic to believer. Once you have passed the "gut test," your personality assets are as real as any hard skill, even to a skeptical listener.

Life events are where evidence of your personality assets is found. Put another way, personality assets are only as valuable as the stories that convince your interviewer you own the asset. Just like mining for diamonds, "mining" your life experiences for personality assets will turn up treasures. Treat your life experiences like valuable gems because, in terms of gaining productive employment, they are your most powerful way to stand out from the crowd.

* * *

Exercise: Start identifying your important life experiences by taking a few moments to answer the following questions regarding *You!*

- What are you doing presently?
- What were you doing before?
- How many years have you been doing what you're doing now?
- Why did you choose this path?
- Where do you want to go from here? Most importantly, Why?

PERSONALITY ASSETS

Next, think back on the times in your life when you learned you were good at something. Maybe a teacher let you know you were particularly creative, thoughtful, or curious. From interactions with friends, you may know that your social skills include being cooperative, diplomatic, or empathic. Perhaps a parent, coach, or pastor has mentioned your maturity level, mentoring skills, or good judgment. Coworkers and managers should be able to identify positive personality qualities that make you stand out from the crowd. Life experiences like these are where personality assets are found. "Mine" your life for the events and experiences that prove you "own" your personality assets.

Use the following list to jog your memory for events and experiences that helped you understand what you are good at.

- School
- Home
- Extracurricular activities
- Hobbies
- Volunteer activities
- Work
- Friends

Depending on the depth of your life experience, you may find you have many, or only a few, experiences illustrating the things you are good at. If you have only a few, don't panic. It's better to have one personality asset with a strong experience substantiating its role in your life than many assets with weak experiences.

* * *

To summarize, the process of identifying personality assets starts by *first* summarizing where you've been, where you're going, and why, because the trajectory of your life events says everything about your values, priorities, and motivations. *Second*, personality assets are found in experiences where you did something well, where you excelled, and typically where someone commented about the asset to you.

As you progress through the Personality Assets system, you will be using all of these experiences to bring your personality assets to life for your interviewer.

Chapter 3

THE FAB IN *YOU!*

Personalizing your interview answers starts with the life experiences identified in the last chapter. Communicating this information in a way that convinces a skeptical interviewer of the importance of the information is the next challenge. The way you tell your story either sells your interviewer on its truthfulness and importance ... or not. A great story isn't just blurted out. To be effective, your story needs to be carefully crafted for its full impact to be understood.

The FAB method is the easiest and best way to tell the story of your personality assets. FAB's start with a factual recounting of a life experience, and go on to state what was accomplished as the result of your personality asset. FAB's end with the benefit you or someone else enjoyed as a result of your accomplishment. Facts and Accomplishments are typically quantitative or measurable. Benefits are qualitative and emphasize your values, priorities, and motivations. FAB's are the backbone of the Personality Assets system.

FAB stands for **Facts**, **A**ccomplishment, **B**enefit:

FAB

- *Facts* -- The Who, What, When, Where, and Why of your life experience. Tell relevant facts, not all the facts.
- *Accomplishment* -- What happened as a result of your Personality Asset. Accomplishments are typically quantitative or measurable.
- *Benefit* -- Your reason for telling this particular story. Benefits are qualitative and speak to what drives you -- your values, priorities, and motivations.

One of the most common errors candidates make during the job interview is to neglect to state the benefit of an accomplishment worth recounting. The listener is left asking themself, "And you told me this because ...?" An Accomplishment without a Benefit is like a birthday cake without candles, the opportunity to celebrate something special has been missed. The results of a job interview are too important to leave the meaning of an important life event up to the imagination of the listener. Even a small Accomplishment can be made *large* with a strong Benefit statement. End every story with a Benefit statement that indicates what drives you, what your priorities are, and gives your listener perspective on what motivates you.

The following are three fictionalized FABs illustrating three different Personality Assets.

The following FAB illustrates the personality asset *can-do*.

Facts: I work on a sales team making telemarketing calls. The work is tough. I get a lot of hang-ups and rejection every day. One day, I came into work wondering if I was cut out for the job. I remembered my interview when I told my boss that I could weather any storm, that I had a real strong can-do attitude. I was wondering if I was wrong, maybe I wasn't as strong as I thought I was. I knew I didn't want to let him down. That day, when I had almost given up, I tried something new. I discovered a trick that changed my results for the better. I found that when the prospect first got on the phone, if I asked permission to take just a few minutes of their time, more people let me complete my pitch—many more! My results were so good that my supervisor asked what I had done differently at the end of the day.

Accomplishments: As a result, my supervisor developed a new script for the team that included asking permission for a few minutes of the prospect's time at the beginning of the call. The team experienced increased numbers of completed calls and increased sales volume, which put more money in everyone's pocket.

Benefits: Morale on the team went up and turnover went down. The company increased our bonus payout because the cost per sale decreased. I was given the Employee of the Month award, which is a pretty big deal at our company, and I'm being considered for a promotion.

The following FAB illustrates the personality asset *outgoing*.

Facts: I am a junior in high school. One day, my art teacher asked me to come to her desk in the middle of class. I thought, *I'm in trouble now* and went over to see what I had done. She told me she was moving me to another table because "there was too much busyness" at the table I was sitting at. In the same breath, she suggested that I should run for class president because "you're so outgoing, you can talk to anyone." I told her I was sorry for any commotion I caused at my old table and that I'd consider her suggestion.

Accomplishments: As a result of my teacher's suggestion, I did run for class president … and won! The kid I ran against had a reputation for being really competitive. I guess he's in the debate club and really smart. The kids in my class all knew me, and I guess they liked me, because they all voted for me. Now I get to represent my class and make decisions that affect us all, and I get up in front of groups and talk about what's going on with the school.

Benefits: I think of myself differently now. I never thought of myself as class president material before my teacher suggested that I run. I see that my teacher was right. I can talk to just about anyone, and that is important when you're making decisions. If you can't talk to people, you don't know what they're thinking.

How can you make good decisions that affect a lot of people if you don't know what the people are thinking? Also, I'm getting a lot of attention from my classmates, even the cheerleaders.

The following FAB illustrates the personality asset *convincing*.

Facts: I joined my company two years ago. It's a small company, and I just got promoted to supervisor. My boss asked me to apply for the supervisor position when it opened up. I was surprised that he asked me, because I hadn't been with the company long. I asked him why he wanted *me* to apply. He told me that the main reason was because I had a way of being convincing, that people listened to me and came around to my way of thinking, even when they didn't agree with me initially. He reminded me of a situation six months ago when corporate came through with an unpopular reorganization. We didn't lose anyone, but everyone's work responsibilities changed. We had nothing to say about it, but it was our job to make it work. A lot of my team members didn't like their new jobs. My boss said he was impressed with how I handled the situation and that things could have gone a lot differently if I hadn't stepped in the way I did. He said I was really good at convincing everyone that the reorg wasn't necessarily bad, that it was important to keep a good attitude, and that things couldn't stay the same forever. He reminded me that I used to say, "Who knows, we might be better off in the long run."

Accomplishments: Corporate wasn't wrong in putting the reorg through. We are working differently, and we may be working harder, but our results are up, way up. In fact, we are doing so well that we're adding six new team members, which is why they created the supervisor position that I just got.

Benefits: My old team members think of themselves like war veterans now. They take pride in the fact they went through the reorg, like it's a badge of honor. They are really a team now, not a grumbling pack of malcontents. With the way our results are going, there'll be plenty of other promotional opportunities coming up, and they're excited about that. The way I see it, everyone won as a result of the reorg.

* * *

Your Job Coach

This book recommends the services of a job coach to prepare you for your job interview. Your job coach rehearses your interview questions and performs mock interviews with you. They have the 360-degree view of your candidacy: they *see* your dress and body language, *hear* your answers, and provide *constructive* feedback. Constructive feedback is objective, includes actionable advice, and is never negative or condemning. For example, "John, you are talking so fast I can't understand every word you're saying. Why don't you try that again. Think about slowing down the speed of your speech. I want to be able to hear every word."

Your job coach can be a volunteer, like a family member or friend; they need not be a professional. You will spend vulnerable moments presenting unrehearsed material to your job coach so choose someone who thinks before they speak and has your best interests at heart.

It is suggested that the following metrics be used to judge the interviewee's performance (3C's + P):

- *Clear*. Can you understand everything the Candidate says? Are words enunciated properly? Are they speaking slowly enough to be understood? Is their answer logical, thorough, and to-the-point?
- *Concise*. Are highly descriptive and targeted words used to convey the most information in a short period of time? Does the Candidate lose their track of thought, ramble, or talk around the point?
- *Consistent*. Is the Candidate's answer internally consistent, or is it contradictory? Is their answer consistent with other answers given to other questions?
- *Persuasive*. Finally, does the answer make you believe that what the Candidate says is true? Is their answer convincing?

If a job coach is not available, or you choose not to use one, you can use other methods to get a third-party perspective on your skill development. Mastering the exercises in this book, combined with a visual check on your performance such as practicing in front of a mirror or videotaping your responses, should produce results similar to what you would gain by working with a job coach.

Exercise: Using one of the soft skills you identified in Chapter 2, apply the FAB approach to communicating your soft skill to your job coach.

Chapter 4

INDIVIDUAL PERSONALITY ASSETS

You are now ready to identify your strongest personality assets. The list of individual assets starts on the next page. Included are words that describe an individual's work product, ethic, attitude, orientation, motivation, and character. This is the largest and, in some ways, the most important dimension because job seekers most often apply for individual contributor roles.

Read each word. If you don't understand a word, skip it and go to the next one. Take your time in reviewing each word. You should find many words that describe your valuable personality assets, possibly more than you imagined!

Choose your five strongest assets from the list on the next page. The assets you choose are the basis for personalizing interview answers regarding suitability to perform the job, work ethic, and motivation for wanting the job.

PERSONALITY ASSETS

Achiever	Good attitude
Accountable	Hard-working
Adaptable	Honest
Analytic	Imaginative
Builder	Industrious
Can-do	Initiator
Clean	Innovative
Common sense	Inquisitive
Conscientious	Intuitive
Consistent	Inventive
Creative	Justice-driven
Critical-thinking	Level-headed
Curious	Loyal
Customer-oriented	Methodical
Decisive	Mission-driven
Dependable	Multi-tasking
Detail-oriented	Neat
Determined	Observant
Disciplined	Open-minded
Doer	Optimistic
Efficient	Organized
Embrace change	Participatory
Embrace learning	Passionate
Energetic	Patient
Enterprising	Perceptive
Expert	Persistent
Fact-based	Planner
Flexible	Positive attitude
Focused	Pragmatic
Follows directions	Precise
Go-getter	Prepared
Goal-oriented	Principled

INDIVIDUAL PERSONALITY ASSETS

Problem-solver
Process-oriented
Punctual
Quick learner
Relentless
Reliable
Resilient
Resourceful
Respectful
Responsive

Results-oriented
Safety-minded
Service-oriented
Stamina
Task-oriented
Tenacious
Thorough
Timely
Tough-minded
Upbeat

Exercise: Circle your five strongest assets and rank them 1 to 5, strongest to weakest. Think of events that illustrate the role the asset played in your life. Apply the FAB approach to tell your story. Rehearse your answer with your job coach.

Chapter 5

SOCIAL PERSONALITY ASSETS

You are now ready to identify your strongest social personality assets. The words starting on the next page describe an individual's interaction style, social and communication skills, and will identify the "fit" between your social personality assets and the culture of the organization you are interviewing with.

As before, take your time in reviewing each word skipping words you don't understand or that don't apply to *You!*

Choose your three strongest assets from the list on the next page. The assets you choose are the basis for personalizing interview answers regarding social needs, interaction style, and conflict resolution skills.

PERSONALITY ASSETS

Apprising	Humble
Booster	Humorous
Cajoling	Independent
Candid	Mannerly
Collaborative	No-nonsense
Collegial	Other-oriented
Compassionate	Outgoing
Competitive	Personable
Congenial	Persuasive
Cooperative	Poised
Deferential	Polished
Diplomatic	Quick-witted
Disclosing	Receptive
Easygoing	Self-aware
Empathic	Spontaneous
Engaging	Straightforward
Egalitarian	Tactful
Forthright	Team player
Gregarious	Trustworthy

Exercise: Circle your three strongest assets and rank them 1 to 3, strongest to weakest. Think of events that illustrate the role the asset played in your life. Apply the FAB approach to tell your story. Rehearse your answer with your job coach.

Chapter 6

LEADERSHIP PERSONALITY ASSETS

The final dimension is leadership personality assets. The words starting on the next page describe qualities that enable an individual to motivate and productively direct the activities of individuals and groups. Leadership personality assets are chosen for their applicability across work environments, understanding that leadership skills are valued quite differently from one work setting to the next.

As before, take your time in reviewing each word skipping words you don't understand or that don't apply to *You!*

Choose your three strongest assets from the list on the next page. The assets you choose are the basis for personalizing interview answers regarding leadership potential, style, and skills.

PERSONALITY ASSETS

- Articulate
- Assertive
- Change agent
- Confident
- Convincing
- Discerning
- Entrepreneurial
- Experienced
- Facilitator
- Fair
- Forward-thinking
- Good judgment
- Influential
- Initiating
- Inspiring
- Mature
- Mediator
- Mentor
- Moderator
- Motivator
- Negotiator
- Persuasive
- Politically-savvy
- Proactive
- Realist
- Respectable
- Responsible
- Self-improving
- Self-motivated
- Self-starter
- Skillful
- Take-charge
- Team building
- Visionary

Exercise: Circle your three strongest and rank them 1 to 3, strongest to weakest. Think of events that illustrate the role the asset played in your life. Apply the FAB approach to tell your story. Rehearse your answer with your job coach.

Chapter 7

TURN A WEAKNESS INTO A STRENGTH

The "Give me a weakness" question is perhaps the toughest question encountered during the job interview. Many candidates never prepare for this question hoping it won't be asked ... and often it isn't! However, when it is, the weakness question offers the prepared candidate a unique opportunity to strengthen their interviewer's resolve to go to the next step by turning a weakness into a strength.

Interviewers ask the weakness question because it's their job to get a 360-degree understanding of your candidacy. They need to determine whether you're a good fit for the position, and understanding the weaknesses of your candidacy is part of that job.

Finding a suitable answer to the weakness question starts by understanding that your interviewer does not expect you to tell them why they shouldn't hire you. The weakness question is best thought of as a *request for information* that reassures your future employer that you are suitable for the position, you will fit in with the organizational culture, and that they are equipped to manage you.

In answering the weakness question, your interviewer deserves an honest appraisal to a legitimate question. A good answer combines strategy with authenticity. Because candidates have more than one weakness, the strategic question comes down to which weakness to share during the interview. Choose the *wrong* weakness and risk not being considered further. Choose the *right* one and strengthen your interviewer's resolve to hire you. And, in order for your weakness answer to be believable, it must be authentically grounded in your life experience, just as your personality assets are believable when grounded in your life experience.

A successful answer will substantiate your interviewer's decision to hire you in one of three ways:

Strength/weakness pair. The "*Superman susceptible to kryptonite*" argument pairs a strength with a weakness making the weakness more acceptable by painting it as the price one pays for the strength. Take your strongest personality asset and think of its downside. When asked the weakness question, start by addressing the asset and then address the downside of the strength. Finally, end with a positive statement about how the strength "overwhelms" the weakness.

> *Example: Methodical/takes longer.* "I hardly ever make mistakes because I'm methodical. However, I can sometimes take longer to do my work than my coworkers. They make fun of me because of the

amount of time I take to get my work done but, when they realize the problems I avoid by getting the work right the first time, I get a lot of respect. My work takes more time upfront, but they have to go back and redo their work, and I hardly ever do."

*　*　*

Acceptable weakness. The *"Supermodel with prima donna complex"* argument addresses a weakness that is familiar to the organization and one they are accustomed to managing. Start by addressing the weakness, then follow up with why you believe it is irrelevant given the job you are applying for. With a little research, you should find that there is least one weakness common to the types of people who perform the job you are seeking. Remember that everyone has weaknesses and the weakness question often comes down to, Is yours one that the employer has experience with and can accommodate? *Also,* this argument can be used to address an obvious weakness irrelevant to the job applied for.

> *Example: Late for work.* "I am late to work, not every day, but more than I'd like. I tend to work late, my average time to get home is 7pm and I sometimes go quite a bit beyond that, and the next morning can be tough. I have found that this isn't unusual for attorneys, so I haven't put much care into changing my habits. Will this be a problem for your firm?"
>
> *Example: Short stays on resume.* I have a series of short stays on my resume. For each job I left, the company either required that I relocate to keep my

title and salary, or I was assigned to a job that I hadn't interviewed for and wasn't suited to. I don't want to keep repeating this pattern. I'm open to opportunities because I know I'm good at what I do, and I like the work. I'm just not willing to relocate. There are enough opportunities locally. I am interviewing today because the opportunity you have is perfect for me. I know that if I get this job, I won't have to relocate, because all your operations are local. I believe I will be productive in the position and will be a loyal employee for as long as you need me.

* * *

Overcoming a weakness. The *"Underdog coming from behind"* argument addresses an obvious shortcoming but turns it into a positive by demonstrating maturity, resolve, problem solving skills, or other personality assets critical to success in the position being applied for. Choosing this argument strengthens a candidacy when the weakness is not trivial and the personality asset illustrated is something the employing organization values. State *what* the weakness was and *why* you decided to do something about it. Describe the *plan* you implemented and the *results* you got or expect.

> *Example: Less than stellar grades. What:* My grades from college are average. *Why:* I put myself through school by working full-time, leaving me less time for studying compared to my classmates. *Plan:* I reduced my expectations of going to medical school because my scholastic record was not competitive. I also know that if I really had wanted to be a doctor,

that I could have taken on debt, something I couldn't talk myself into. *Results:* I took the financial experience I gained in college and became an accountant. My aversion to debt is appreciated in the accounting industry, and my grades didn't hold me back.

* * *

It's not uncommon for the first weakness that comes to mind to not fit any of these three strategies. *This is a red flag.* Choosing the right weakness is tricky ... and important. Most of us have more than one weakness, and perhaps most of these weaknesses will never be turned into a strength.

Exercise: Review your weaknesses with your job coach. Think each weakness through carefully for implications that might not occur to you immediately. Think of new weaknesses until you find one that reinforces the strengths of your candidacy. Spend the time necessary to find the weakness that strengthens your interviewer's resolve to hire you.

* * *

If you are not able to fit *any* of your weaknesses into one of the strategies above, you may want to reconsider the jobs you are applying for. Perhaps they are not well suited to *You!*

Chapter 8

YOUR ELEVATOR PITCH

A useful exercise for any job candidate is to compose a short summary of what your job search is all about. Getting crystal clear on the high points of the job search forces the candidate to commit to its critical elements and gives clarity and direction to the search.

This short summary of your job search is colloquially called your "elevator pitch." It comes in handy during the job interview when you are asked the "Tell me about yourself" question. Your elevator pitch should be short enough for a 60-second elevator ride but long enough to be informative. A good elevator pitch includes the following:

1. Number of years of experience you have.
2. The nature of the experience relevant to the job you are looking for.

3. Relevant personality assets.
4. What you are looking for in a job.

Most people speak 180-200 words in one minute. Here's an example of a thirty-second elevator pitch (90 words).

> "I'm a twenty-year business professional who for the last ten years has been self-employed as a one-man provider of executive recruiting services to the health actuarial community. As a small business person, I have developed a broad range of skills ranging from budgeting to operations to marketing. I'm an initiator and I don't shrink from a challenge. I have a cooperative and collaborative work style, although I typically work independently. I am looking for a leadership position with an organization in need of business acumen, and entrepreneurial spirit and know-how."

Remember Nick Flynn from the introduction, the young man who wanted to work at the homeless shelter? He fumbled the job interview the first time but eventually got the job and was successful at it. Nick's elevator speech would have gone something like this (107 words).

> "I'm at a point in my life where I am just starting out. I've worked a few part-time jobs but nothing that's meant much to me. Right now, I have a need to reach out and be helpful to others. I feel that I am a compassionate person, and patient, but I can also be tough-minded, so I think I'll be able to handle some of the tougher clients served at the homeless

shelter. I feel like I have something to contribute to people's lives, and at the end of the day, I think this job would allow me to help others while feeling good about myself."

If Nick had been prepared with this elevator pitch when he first interviewed for the homeless shelter job, he would not have had to rely on luck or serendipity to get the job.

* * *

Exercise: Write down your elevator pitch, practice it, then test it on job coach. If he doesn't "hear" what you *mean* to say, rework your pitch in light of the feedback. Developing your elevator pitch gives clarity and direction to your job search by forcing you to simplify and commit to its elements.

Chapter 9

ADVANCED PERSONALITY ASSETS: ANY QUESTIONS?

A standard question toward the latter part of the job interview is "Do you have any questions for me?" Many candidates are worn out by this part of the interview and do not take advantage of the opportunity presented by this question.

The "Any questions" question is most likely the first time in the interview that you are given the opportunity to take the lead in the conversation. Up until now, the interviewer has been in control asking questions and eliciting answers from you. This is your opportunity to take the lead and stand out from the crowd! Make yourself shine by presenting additional personality assets that the interviewer could only dream of finding in a job applicant! Lackluster or losing candidacies can be turned into winning ones at this point in the interview.

Interviewers are genuinely interested in the questions you bring to the interview because, not only do they provide insight into your motivations and priorities, but they allow the interviewer to provide you with information you are lacking, information you need to decide whether this is the right opportunity for you. The decision to take a job is a two-way street and good candidates are hard to get. Part of the interviewer's job is to sell good candidates on their company, and this involves getting you the information you need about the position, the company, and the industry to make a decision to choose them. Demonstrate your professionalism by using the "Any questions" question to connect with your interviewer and turn the interview into a truly productive two-way forum.

Come to the interview prepared for the "Any questions?" question. In putting your questions together, think about the direction your questions will take the interview. Your questions should lead the conversation in the direction of personality assets that you haven't had a chance to address. If you only come armed with questions about vacation days and benefits, this leads the interviewer to question your work ethic. Questions about the priorities of the company, how the work is performed, what makes for successful working relationships, how success is measured, how resources are allocated, career track, or how decisions are made, *when related with relevant personality assets*, are a powerful way to differentiate yourself from the crowd and will lead one step closer to the job offer.

In the following example, the candidate asks a question about how much travel the job entails. The personality asset he chooses to illustrate is *gregarious*.

> "I appreciate your time in clarifying my question about the out-of-town work schedule. I know that

developing and maintaining relationships in this line of work is critical to success, and the amount of travel you mentioned is reasonable. I'm a gregarious person and I enjoy meeting people. My boss at my last job was pleased that I spent as much time as I did out of the office, because I always seemed to make the sales. He couldn't account for my every minute, but I always produced for him. I have a strong family, and they appreciate the sacrifice I make in providing for them, so there's no issue there."

* * *

You know you're on your "A-game" when you take the lead during the latter part of the interview and demonstrate additional personality assets. This builds confidence in your candidacy on the part of your interviewer that may just win you the job offer. Using the "Any questions?" question to sell additional personality assets qualifies you for "A-game" pro status.

Exercise: Review your personality assets inventory. Think of questions you can ask an interviewer that will act as a bridge to an asset you have yet to introduce.

Chapter 10

BRINGING IT ALL TOGETHER: THE JOB INTERVIEW

This chapter tells the fictionalized, third-person story of an accountant applying for a job with a local competitor. The interview questions used in this chapter are not representative of the broad spectrum of questions that could be asked during an interview, but are typical questions used to probe soft skills where personality assets are relevant.

Two narratives are given for each question: the first where the job candidate *has not* received Personality Assets training, the second where he *has*. Notes are provided that evaluate both answers to each question. Pay close attention to identify the role Personality Assets plays in the performance of the second job candidate.

* * *

To begin ...

You walk into the job interview feeling confident and prepared. You have memorized the job description, reviewed most of the available company-related information, and know that your hard skills match the job requirements perfectly. Your interviewer walks into the room, shakes your hand, sits down, and begins by commenting that you're both from the same State. You relax, knowing that the first few moments of any interview are the toughest.

Question:
"Tell me about yourself."

WITHOUT PERSONALITY ASSETS

You knew this question would come up but it wasn't at the top of your list to prepare for. You spent more time than you expected last night reviewing the company's financials.

"I have five years experience directly related to the position. I'm really interested in this job because it represents a step forward for me in terms of responsibilities. I am a hard-working, goal-oriented person and am looking for my next challenge."

You feel pretty good. Everything you said was true, and the interviewer looks satisfied.

WITH PERSONALITY ASSETS

You are prepared with your elevator pitch for this question.

"I'm a five-year tax accountant employed by Curley & Moe. I worked my way through college and found that numbers came easily to me so decided to go into accounting. I enjoy my work. I get a lot of kudos because I am very goal-oriented and conscientious. I'm currently open to opportunities because I feel like I'm ready for the next step in my career, and manager positions don't open up very often at Curely & Moe. I saw your ad and thought I'd give it a shot."

PERSONALITY ASSETS

Note: Although the candidate *without* Personality Assets does a good job of thinking on his feet, the candidate *with* Personality Assets conveyed more information in roughly the same period of time because he was prepared with his elevator pitch.

* * *

Question:
"Tell me a time when you worked really hard to achieve a sought-after goal."

WITHOUT PERSONALITY ASSETS

Your mind is racing. You hadn't prepared for this question and you think, *When was the last time I put in overtime at work?*

"Last tax season we had a big deadline, and I must have put in two eighty-hour weeks in a row. It was crazy, but we made the deadline. My boss was pretty happy about how things turned out."

You breathe a sigh of relief, having dodged a bullet. You think, *When is he going to ask about my technical skills?*

WITH PERSONALITY ASSETS

Your strongest personality assets are goal-oriented and conscientious, and you've identified recent examples of both.

"My boss tries to manage the work during tax season so we don't have to pull all-nighters, and he's usually pretty good at it, but last year we had a couple of clients with more work than we expected. A lot more. I ended up putting in a couple of eighty-hour weeks in a row. We were all working hard to get the work done and keep the client happy. It was pretty crazy, but we did it. That's the important thing."

Note: The candidate *without* Personality Assets makes a good argument regarding his work performance. The candidate *with* Personality Assets demonstrates an understanding of the pressures his manager is under, as well as making a good argument for his work performance.

* * *

Question:
"Tell me about when you were putting in those long hours and things were a little tense. How did you handle it?"

WITHOUT PERSONALITY ASSETS

Your mind is fraying. *Why is he asking me this?* You remember last tax season when your coworker was behind on his reconciliations. It was late, and you were tired. You gruffly told him you'd do the reconciliations if he couldn't. You were at the office until three in the morning getting it done.

"Last year, a coworker was behind on his work. I offered to do his work because I couldn't do mine until his was done. I was at the office until three in the morning getting it all done. It was really hard, but at least it got done."

WITH PERSONALITY ASSETS

You're unprepared for this question, and your mind races, but you remember the weakness exercise.

"Last tax season, we got the work done on time, but I wasn't communicating well with my boss. After those couple of eighty-hour weeks, he asked me why I was putting in so much overtime. We had a heart-to-heart, and I told him about the coworker who was behind on his reconciliations. I felt uncomfortable mentioning my coworker's shortcomings, but it didn't help my boss to not tell him. Does that answer your question?"

PERSONALITY ASSETS

Note: The candidate *without* Personality Assets does a good job under the circumstances by giving an authentic answer. The candidate *with* Personality Assets excels because he is prepared with a thoughtful answer demonstrating the ability to embrace change.

* * *

Question:
"Have you applied for management positions with your current company?"

WITHOUT PERSONALITY ASSETS

This is a sore point. You recently applied for a management position and the interview went well, but you didn't get the job. The guy who got it was the coworker whose reconciliations you completed at three in the morning. Obviously, your boss recommended him over you. You feel your face flush.

"I did apply recently for a management position. I didn't get it. I wasn't given a reason why."

WITH PERSONALITY ASSETS

"Yes, I did. I lost out to the guy whose work I did until three in the morning. At first I couldn't understand why he got it, but then it dawned on me that I was rejected because I didn't communicate effectively with my manager. I didn't tell him about the backlog of work. I should have. Since I got turned down for manager, I've been working on my communication skills and am trying to be more forthright with my boss."

Note: The candidate *without* Personality Assets is not prepared for an emotionally charged question. The candidate *with* Personality Assets excels again because he has thought through important issues affecting his career performance. He gives an answer that demonstrates self-knowledge, humility, and honesty.

* * *

Question:
"Any questions for me?"

WITHOUT PERSONALITY ASSETS

"No. I think you've answered all my questions."

WITH PERSONALITY ASSETS

"Yes. I consider myself to be pretty outgoing compared to a lot of the guys I work with. I think I could be good at business development some day. What is the career track here?"

The rest of the interview goes pretty well.

Note: The candidate *without* Personality Assets surrendered the opportunity to direct the interview by being unprepared with questions that bridged to an additional personality asset. This represented his last chance at salvaging the interview. The candidate *with* Personality Assets excels again because he is prepared with a question and a personality asset.

* * *

In conclusion ...

WITHOUT PERSONALITY ASSETS

You find out you didn't get the job, and no reason is given. You are frustrated and wonder if there's something you did wrong. The interviewer's private evaluation notes read, "The candidate lacks an understanding of why his career is stalled at Curley & Moe. Therefore, the candidate is unprepared for the next level of responsibility."

WITH PERSONALITY ASSETS

You find out that you have been offered the job, and you accept. The interviewer's private evaluation notes reads, "The candidate has a realistic understanding of his past job performance at Curley & Moe and has taken steps to address challenges to his management skill set. Candidate demonstrates a level of maturity appropriate to the responsibilities of the manager position."

* * *

As the above fictionalized account illustrates, the candidate with Personality Assets presented a compelling summary of his candidacy, sold his soft skill strengths, turned a weakness into a strength, and finally, turned the "Any questions" question into an additional sales venue, qualifying him for "A-game" pro status. The Personality Assets system works by preparing job candidates with the tools they need to differentiate themselves from the crowd and get the job they deserve.

Chapter 11

YOUR MOCK JOB INTERVIEW

Now is your chance to apply your interviewing tools to a mock interview situation. In this role-play scenario, your job coach plays Interviewer and you play Interviewee.

Your Interviewer will use the following script to guide the interview. The script addresses interview questions that are relevant to personality assets. In a real interview, you will most likely get additional questions that address your job history and hard skills.

* * *

Begin Interview

Interviewee: Walk toward your job coach. Look her straight in the eye and shake her hand firmly. Sit down.

Interviewer: "Thanks for coming in today. My name is _____ and you are interviewing for the (<u>Dream Job</u>) position we have open. How was the traffic coming over today?"

Interviewee answers the ice-breaker question.

Interviewer: "Okay, let's get started. Did you bring a copy of your resume? Thanks."

1. "Tell me about yourself."
2. "What are your strengths?"
3. "How do you see yourself fitting in here?"
4. "Do you have any experiences you can tell me about that might help me understand your work habits, how you relate to coworkers, and what kind of initiative you've taken in the past?"
5. "What are your weaknesses?"
6. "Why do you want to work here?"
7. "Any questions for me?"

Interviewer: (Stand up and shake the Interviewee's hand) "Thanks for coming in. We'll decide in the next few days who we'll be hiring. If we decide to pursue your candidacy, what's the best way to get a hold of you?"

* * *

Job Coach: Interviewer Comments

Did the Interviewee seem relaxed?

Did he look you in the eye?

Was his handshake firm?

Was the answer to "Tell me about yourself" concise and complete? Did the Interviewee use his elevator pitch?

Were the Interviewee's strengths relevant to the job?

Did the Interviewee have a realistic sense of the workplace and how he might fit into the organization?

Did the Interviewee address his personality assets in a way that was relevant and convincing?

How did the weakness question go? Was the Interviewee able to turn the weakness into a strength?

Was the Interviewee prepared for the "Why do you want to work here" question? Was his answer convincing?

Did the Interviewee have questions at the end that made sense in terms of the rest of the interview?

Did the Interviewee insert a relevant personality asset after asking his questions?

PERSONALITY ASSETS

Did you like the Interviewee?

Did you think the Interviewee was honest?

Did you think the Interviewee was qualified?

Would you hire this Interviewee?

What improvements could you recommend?

_____

Initials/Date

FINAL THOUGHTS

There's no getting around the fact that interviewing for a job involves a certain amount of drama. Preparing for the interview is like rehearsing for a play. You learn your lines, and practice them for their best effect. The onsite interview is like the first night's performance: the curtain goes up, the interview begins, and you give it all you've got. The results of the interview—job offer or rejection—are like the critics' next-day reviews. You're either a raving success or a flop.

The Personality Assets system equips you with the analytical framework and substantive tools to personalize your interview answers and get you to your "A-game" during the job interview. When you perform well, you're able to accept the results of any job interview, whether it's job offer or rejection, without regrets or second guessing. The interviewing process is less about winning or losing, and more about finding where your strengths are valued and where your weaknesses are acceptable. Look at rejection as information you didn't have before the interview.

Armed with this information, you may decide to take your job search in a different direction, or to get more serious about reaching your "A-game."

Although its contents are simple, you'll find you won't master the material in this book overnight. Pat answers don't get you very far in the job interview, as you may have already found out the hard way. The analytical framework and substantive tools developed in this book *will* help you find your most persuasive argument for being the *right* person and *best* candidate for the job, but sometimes a large dose of patience is required. Keep at it and the insights will follow. Your perseverance will be rewarded!

Make your Personality Assets a touchstone. Commit to keeping your inventory current and take your career as far as it's meant to go. Use this book to confidently approach your next job interview and *get the job you deserve*!

Appendix

PERSONALITY ASSETS

Individual		**Social**	**Leadership**
Achiever	Customer-oriented	Apprising	Articulate
Accountable		Booster	Assertive
Adaptable	Decisive	Cajoling	Change agent
Analytic	Dependable	Candid	Confident
Builder	Detail-oriented	Collaborative	Convincing
Can-do	Determined	Collegial	Discerning
Clean	Disciplined	Compassionate	Entrepreneurial
Common sense	Doer	Competitive	Experienced
	Efficient	Congenial	Facilitator
Conscientious	Embrace change	Cooperative	Fair
Consistent		Deferential	Forward-thinking
Creative	Embrace learning	Diplomatic	
Critical thinking		Disclosing	Good judgment
	Energetic	Easygoing	Influential
Curious	Enterprising	Empathic	Initiating

PERSONALITY ASSETS

- Expert
- Fact based
- Flexible
- Focused
- Follow directions
- Go-getter
- Goal-oriented
- Good attitude
- Hard-working
- Honest
- Imaginative
- Industrious
- Initiator
- Innovative
- Inquisitive
- Intuitive
- Inventive
- Justice-driven
- Level-headed
- Loyal
- Methodical
- Mission-driven
- Multi-tasking
- Neat
- Observant
- Open-minded
- Optimistic
- Organized
- Participatory
- Passionate
- Patient
- Perceptive
- Persistent
- Planner
- Positive attitude
- Pragmatic
- Precise
- Prepared
- Principled
- Problem solver
- Process-oriented
- Punctual
- Quick learner
- Relentless
- Reliable
- Resilient
- Resourceful
- Respectful
- Responsive
- Results-oriented
- Safety-minded
- Service-oriented
- Stamina
- Task oriented
- Tenacious
- Thorough
- Timely
- Tough-minded
- Upbeat
- Engaging
- Egalitarian
- Forthright
- Gregarious
- Humble
- Humorous
- Independent
- Mannerly
- No-nonsense
- Other-oriented
- Outgoing
- Personable
- Persuasive
- Poised
- Polished
- Quick-witted
- Receptive
- Self-aware
- Spontaneous
- Straightforward
- Tactful
- Team player
- Trustworthy
- Inspiring
- Mature
- Mediator
- Mentor
- Moderator
- Motivator
- Negotiator
- Persuasive
- Politically savvy
- Proactive
- Realist
- Respectable
- Responsible
- Self-improving
- Self-motivated
- Self-starter
- Skillful
- Take charge
- Team building
- Visionary

GLOSSARY

360-degree view: An all encompassing view. In the case of the job interview, the perspective of the interviewer that includes how the job candidate looks, sounds, and the overall impression made.

Acceptable weakness: Strategy for turning a weakness into a strength. A familiar weakness for the job or industry; one that the organization is accustomed to managing.

Candidate: Job seeker; an individual who has applied for a job.

Chemistry: What happens during a job interview when an interviewer recognizes a match between the soft needs of an organization and the soft skills of a candidate.

Dimensions: Schema that allows personality assets to be categorized according to the level of analysis applied. Dimensions address fundamental aspects of work life: individual, social, and leadership.

Facts, Accomplishments, and Benefits (FAB): Three-step method of telling a story that includes the benefit of actions taken and why the story is important.

Hard skills: Quantifiable job skills that a person acquires through education, experience, or training.

Individual personality assets: Reflect the various ways individuals contribute to a work environment. They describe an individual's work product, ethic, attitude, orientation, style, motivation, and character.

Job coach: Person who role plays job interviews and gives honest feedback about interview performance.

Leadership personality assets: Qualities that enable an individual to motivate and productively direct the activities of individuals and groups. Leadership personality assets are chosen for their applicability across work environments, understanding that leadership skills that are valuable in one work setting may not be equally valued in a different work setting.

Leverage: During the job interview, the use of a strength to its greatest advantage to obtain the candidate's desired outcome.

Mock interview: A pretend interview where a candidate practices for a real interview.

GLOSSARY

Overcoming a weakness: Strategy for turning a weakness into a strength. Demonstrates a strength, like maturity or self-management, through the overcoming of a weakness.

Personality Assets: Subset of soft skills that are relevant to the workplace, highly descriptive, and valued across varying work environments. Personality assets are divided into three dimensions—Individual, Social, and Leadership—for ease of application.

Social personality assets: Includes personality assets that describe your interaction style, social skills, communication skills, and how you relate with coworkers.

Soft skills: Personality characteristics that can't be seen or measured but are real and valuable.

Strength/weakness pair: Strategy for turning a weakness into a strength. A weakness is mitigated by first introducing its upside, a strength, thereby positioning the weakness as the price one pays for the strength.

***You!*:** The combination of all the soft skills you "own." The exponential relationship between number of soft skills and their unique combinations means that the probability that every human being is unique, vis-à-vis soft skills, is high.

ABOUT THE AUTHOR

Leslie Macomber is a twenty-year business professional. Ms. Macomber is President of Health Actuary Search, Inc., an executive recruiting firm specializing in the placement of health actuaries. Her passion is helping job candidates find satisfying employment and the efficient deployment of human capital skills. She holds an MBA from the University of California at Berkeley and a BA in Behavioral Science from the University of Chicago. Leslie lives with her husband and two children in Coeur d'Alene, Idaho.

www.ingramcontent.com/pod-product-compliance
Lightning Source LLC
Chambersburg PA
CBHW061516180526
45171CB00001B/201